Roots

By
Gemma McMullen

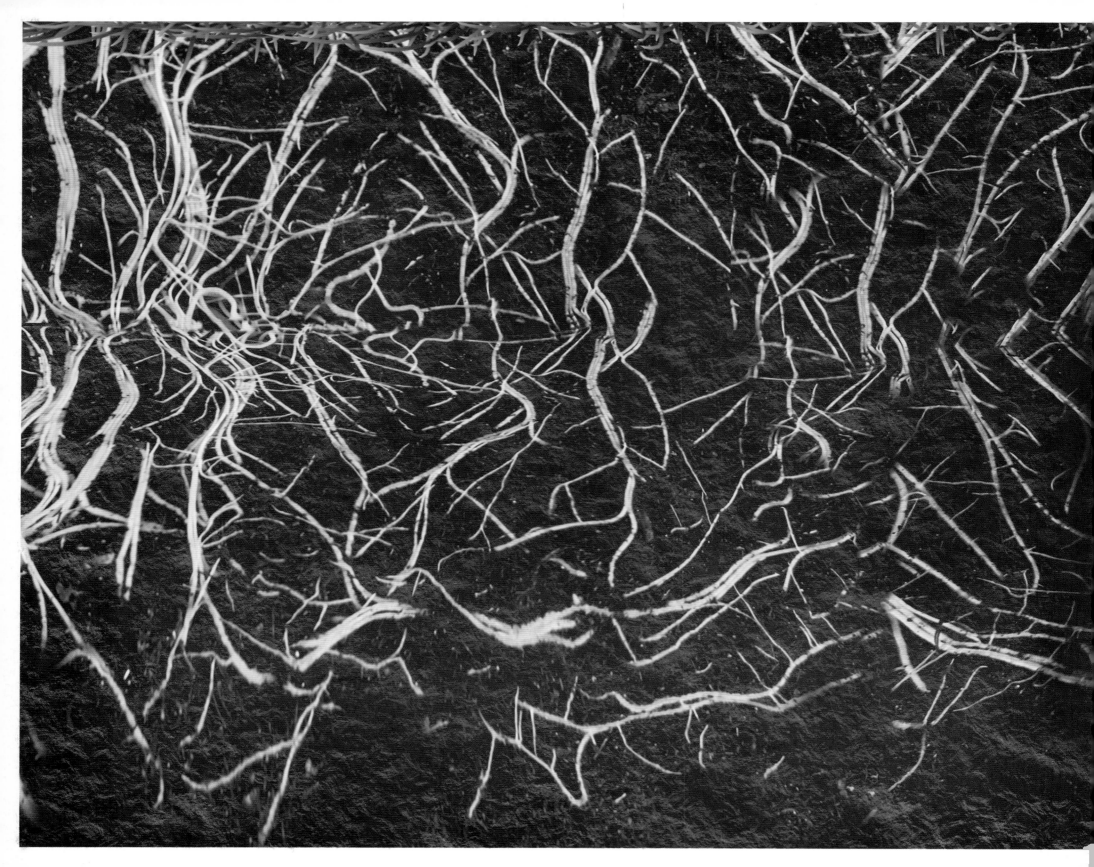

Contents

©2016
Book Life
King's Lynn
Norfolk PE30 4LS

ISBN: 978-1-910512-53-1

All rights reserved
Printed in China
A catalogue record for
this book is available
from the British Library.

Written by
Gemma McMullen

Edited by
Harriet Brundle

Designed by
Ian McMullen

Words in colour like *this* can be found in the glossary on page 24.

What is a Plant?

A plant is a living thing. Trees, shrubs, flowers and weeds are all plants. People and animals need plants to live.

A Plant

4

Sunlight

Plants need water, sunlight and heat to live. They make their own food using energy from the sun.

What are Roots?

Roots

All plants have different parts. The roots are part of a plant. Most, but not all, plants have roots.

Small
Roots

Some roots are very large but others are much smaller. Many roots grow under the ground, making them difficult to see.

Large Tree Roots

What do Roots look Like?

Roots come in many different shapes and sizes. They can be different colours too.

Beetroot

Acorn Tree Roots

Daffodil Roots

The roots of an acorn tree are very large. They go very deep underground.

The roots of a daffodil are much smaller and are white.

9

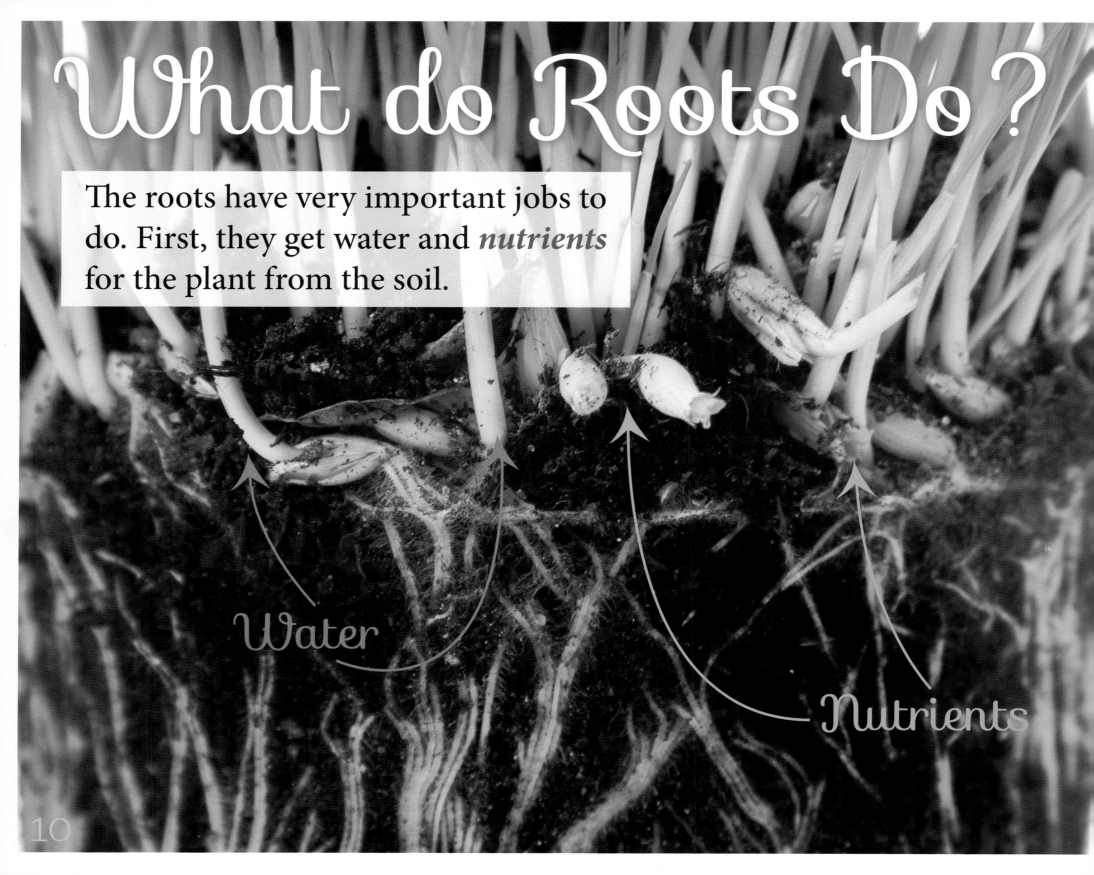

What do Roots Do?

The roots have very important jobs to do. First, they get water and *nutrients* for the plant from the soil.

Water

Nutrients

Secondly, roots help to keep plants firmly in the ground.
Without roots, a plant could blow over in the wind.

What else do Roots Do?

As well as taking from the soil, plant roots also help the soil. Plant roots help to keep the soil in place when it is raining.

When soil is washed away it can cause *mudslides*. Mudslides can be dangerous for people and animals.

13

How do People use Roots?

Some roots are *edible* for humans, which means that they can be eaten. Can you think of any plant roots that people eat?

Carrots

Potatoes

Carrots are actually the roots of the carrot plant. Potatoes are also plant roots.

How do Animals use Roots?

Rabbit

Roots are food to some animals that live underground.
Rabbits have been known to dig up carrots in farmers' fields.

Animals, such as moles, bite through roots when digging underground, which can cause damage to the plant.

Mole

Where do Roots Grow?

An Orchid's Roots

18

Many plants have roots that grow underneath the ground, but some plant roots grow above the ground.

Mistletoe

Mistletoe grows on trees. Its roots break into the tree's bark so that the mistletoe can share the tree's nutrients.

Do all Plants have Roots?

Not all plants have roots. Mosses grow in damp places and take water in from the air around them.

Moss

Instead of roots, seaweed has *holdfasts* which keep it on the sea floor. Holdfasts do not take in water and nutrients.

Holdfasts

Seaweed

21

Root-filled Facts!

Roots Rock!

Roots help to make soil! They break rocks into small pieces which later becomes soil.

Root Wreckage

Large tree roots growing underground have been known to lift pavements and damage brick walls.

Hairy Roots!

The parts of the roots which take in the water are called the root hairs.

23

Glossary

edible can be eaten safely

holdfasts how seaweed attaches itself

mudslides a large amount of mud that has fallen down a slope

nutrients the food needed for growth and health

Index

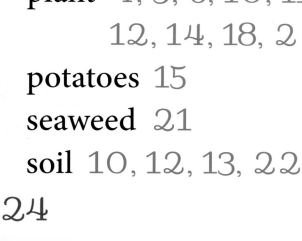